trade justice

a Christian response to global poverty

W0009345

...ort by Christian Aid

CHURCH HOUSE PUBLISHING

Church House Publishing
Church House
Great Smith Street
London
SW1P 3NZ
Tel. 020 7898 1451
Fax 020 7898 1449

ISBN 0 7151 4047 7

Published 2004 by Church House Publishing.

GS Misc 744

*This report was commissioned from Christian Aid by
the Church of England's Mission and Public Affairs
Council as a contribution to the debate at General
Synod and beyond about trade justice issues.*

The Scripture quotations contained herein are from
the New Revised Standard Version Bible, copyright
© 1989, by the Division of Christian Education of
the National Council of the Churches of Christ in the
USA, and are used by permission. All rights reserved.

Cover design by Church House Publishing

Printed in England by Halstan & Co. Ltd,
Amersham, Bucks

contents

preface

As we enter the twenty-first century, we live in a world where poverty and inequality have reached unprecedented levels. Current international trade rules are failing to alleviate this situation and in many places are actually making things much worse.

Responding to God's call to work for justice in the world, the Church has a responsibility to be at the forefront of moves to transform the world, rid it of poverty and make it a more just and equitable place for all people. There are many ways in which the Church seeks to do this, including prayer, and raising money to fund development and relief work throughout the world. But one of the most important is in supporting the growing international campaign for trade justice.

The year 2005 has the potential to be a vital one for development issues. The UK Government will host the G8 leaders' summit in summer 2005 and will also hold the presidency of the European Union during the latter half of the year. This gives the Government the opportunity to shape the international agenda. The Prime Minister has already launched an international commission to propose solutions to Africa's problems, which will report in advance of the G8 summit, and has underlined his Government's commitment to further progress towards the Millennium Development Goals for poverty eradication. Faith groups and development agencies are talking about how they can influence this process.

It is essential that far-reaching changes in international trade rules accompany any promises to increase finance to poor countries. The impact of changes in trade policy could be massive. Even under current trade rules, poor countries earn US$400 billion every year from trade,[1] eight times what they receive in aid each year, and equivalent to four times the total debt relief promised by the G8 in Cologne in 1999.

Trade policy has long been the preserve of expert economists and has rarely been the subject of popular debate. But it is so fundamental to moves to eradicate poverty that it cannot be ignored any longer. Together we must listen to God's call and be ready to speak out and campaign for a more just world.

✠ John Gladwin
Bishop of Chelmsford
Chair of the Board of Christian Aid

acknowledgements

This report was written by Mary Bradford, Justin Macmullan and Claire Melamed, and edited by Jane Lewis, on behalf of Christian Aid, for the Mission and Public Affairs Council of the Church of England. Many of the ideas in the theology chapter were developed after a workshop with Andrew Bradstock, Bishop Michael Doe, Peter Graystone, Leslie Nathaniel, Elizabeth Perry, Jennifer Potter, Bishop Peter Selby, Hannah Skinner, Graham Sparkes, Wendy Tyndale and Nigel Varndell. Several of these people also provided further comments on the text, for which we are grateful. Additional comments were received from Martin Drewry, Liz Dodd, Fiona Gooch, David Pain, Andy Redfern, Charles Reed and Roger Riddell.

Onion farmers in Senegal, like Bolo Sy, are struggling to make a living from trade.

Christian Aid/Harriet Logan/Network

chapter one

introduction to trade

poverty, inequality and trade

At the beginning of the twenty-first century the world is more unequal than it has ever been. Three rich individuals control more wealth than the whole of sub-Saharan Africa. In 1970, the richest 20 per cent of the world's people had 32 times the income of the poorest 20 per cent. By 1999, this group had 78 times the income of the poorest group.[1] While, on average, people in the UK earn more than £60 per day, more than half of the world's population survives on less than £1.20 per day.

While there are many factors contributing to this growing inequality (conflict, disease, pandemics such as HIV/AIDS, international debt and others), the way in which international trade operates is among the most significant. After all, trade is fundamental to the growth of economies and so provides direct income for businesses as well as for individuals, and, through taxation, money to fund public services, education, healthcare and infrastructure.

International trade is governed by rules negotiated between countries at the World Trade Organization (WTO). Other international institutions, such as the International Monetary Fund (IMF) and World Bank, also have great influence – particularly over the way poor countries trade. Because of their much greater wealth and power, rich countries tend to dominate these international bodies. As will be suggested in this report, these rules and agreements are systematically biased against the interests of poor communities and poor countries.

The Church cannot stand and watch this situation develop and deteriorate without seeking to do everything in its power to change it. The Christian community needs to make the gospel values of justice, fairness and hope heard among international decision-makers. It needs to win support for a different way of doing things, one that puts the needs of the poorest people, and the demands of justice, first.

globalization and the growth of trade

The process of globalization, which increasingly connects individuals around the world, has been both a driver and a consequence of the increase in global trade. Consumers can now buy products assembled in Eastern Europe, from parts manufactured in east Asia, made of raw materials mined in Africa. Individuals can telephone a call centre and find themselves talking to someone in India, or hold an email conversation with a friend in Latin America.

As part of this process of globalization, international trade has undeniably been an engine for growth in the developed, and some parts of the developing, world. It has brought the benefits of jobs and technology as well as goods and services. Standards of living have continued to improve.

However, for those on the other side of the 'divide' the story has been very different. For example, African economies are increasingly dependent on unpredictable trade relationships, in which Africa is losing out in comparison with other developing countries, as well as with developed countries. Whereas Africa accounted for 6 per cent of the world's exports in 1980, this fell to just 2 per cent in 2002.[2] In 2001, the value of exports from the whole of sub-Saharan Africa was just 9 per cent higher than that of Switzerland.

faced with the reality

On our way up north we saw some onion farmers. I met Fatima, who works 12 hours a day in the 40-degree heat with a baby strapped on her back, for £1.50 a week. She was angry, not at the weight of her toil, but that the price of the onions she farmed was being brought so low by the subsidized ones imported from Holland. She would soon not be able to survive, no matter how many hours she worked in the sun.

Suddenly she stopped, looked into my eyes and asked if she could pray for me. She blessed me – me, from the rich west – blessed me. I was so profoundly affected by this that I sat in silence for the remainder of our four-hour journey north to Njum.

Excerpt from a report written by Kwame Kwei-Armah, actor and playwright, following a Christian Aid trip to Senegal.

The experience of onion farmers in Senegal (see above) sums up the problem for many. Under international pressure, the Senegalese Government opened its markets to international trade. This pitched the onion farmers into competition with producers from Holland – where most of the European onions originate. These European producers have the technology to store their produce, and also receive compensation from the European Commission if the price they receive falls below a certain level. In contrast, Senegalese farmers struggle with outdated technology, crumbling infrastructure and little or no support from their government.

Such cases are typical of many across Africa, Central America and south Asia. While, on an international scale, the growth in trade and the increased use of fossil fuels raise questions about environmental sustainability, for people who are already desperately poor, trade is not providing the lifeline that it should.

trade and justice

To even a casual reader of the Bible, this situation might, perhaps, not be so surprising. The biblical writers, particularly in the Old Testament, warn again and again that, unless trade is accompanied by measures to ensure justice, it all too easily slips into exploitation. The words of the prophet Amos, written in the eighth century BC, ring down the years:

> Hear this, you that trample on the needy, and bring to ruin the poor of the land, saying 'When will the new moon be over so that we may sell grain; and the sabbath, so that we may offer wheat for sale?
> We will make the ephah small and the shekel great, and practise deceit with false balances.'
>
> Amos 8.4-5

According to Amos, such exploitation is condemned by God – as is equivalent exploitation taking place today.

So can trade be good and can it be made to work in the interests of poor people? The answer to both questions is certainly 'yes'. Trade – an exchange of goods or services between two parties – can be something that enriches both. It is the *exploitation* that Amos condemns, not the trade itself – the 'poor of the land' in his time (possibly landless themselves) needed to buy grain and wheat to eat and, without the merchants to sell these crops to them, they would have starved.

The fact that trade can serve the interests of both parties is shown through the modern fair-trade movement, where producers in the developing world are paid a premium above the world-market price for consumer products such as tea, coffee and cocoa. Consumers get good-quality products and producers get price stability and a guaranteed market. The fair-trade premiums paid to these communities have contributed to building local schools and health centres and to investment in production and marketing.

This type of trade is still only a tiny proportion of the global total, but it offers hope that an alternative is possible. However, the bigger challenge is to transform the rules that govern all international trade so that they are weighted to benefit poor communities.

With this kind of international support, trade could offer real hope for some of the poorest countries in the world. As discussed further below (p. 23), there are instances where this has already happened. Mauritius, a tiny island in the Indian Ocean, used to be almost totally dependent on one product – sugar. Its people were poor, trapped in an economy with few alternatives. But, between 1975 and 1999, national growth per person averaged 4.2 per cent and productivity increased. More importantly, inequality fell and life expectancy increased by ten years.

This, however, will not be repeated on a global scale unless there are major changes to the rules that govern international trade. At the moment, these rules are increasingly forcing poor countries to adopt a 'one-size-fits-all' policy of trade 'liberalization'. This policy severely limits the ability of poor countries to use the tools that rich countries have used in the past (and still use) to build and maintain competitive advantage and so reap the benefits of expanding world trade.

In particular:

- world leaders must stop forcing poor countries to open their markets to international trade;
- poor countries must be allowed the flexibility to give special help to their farmers and industries so they can reduce poverty and help new, productive sectors to develop.

Only then will trade rules be truly weighted in favour of poor communities.

building the Trade Justice Campaign

To achieve such far-reaching change on an international scale needs political will among those in positions of power and influence. Working together with organizations in developing countries, campaigners in the UK need to build a campaign of massive and unprecedented proportions that will hold leaders accountable for the decisions they make on our behalf.

The Jubilee 2000 campaign for the cancellation of poor countries' debts showed how it was possible to change opinion and policy on major international issues. By developing a popular campaign that made the issues accessible to many people, the pressure on international decision-makers was built to such a level that they had to act. They have not yet delivered on all the campaign's demands, but the achievements were still significant.

As the year 2005 approaches, attention is increasingly focusing on the Millennium Development Goals. These eight goals were adopted in 2000 and aim to eradicate extreme poverty and hunger by the year 2015. But five years on from when they were agreed, it is becoming increasingly obvious that, without major changes, the goals will not be achieved.

Now is the time to mobilize political will towards achieving these goals. International aid must be increased and a much greater proportion of poor countries' debts must be cancelled. But, for these measures to have a lasting impact, there must also be major changes to the way international trade is managed.

Learning the lessons from Jubilee 2000, the Trade Justice Campaign must illuminate the obscure world of international trade rules and lay the blatant injustices open for all to see. When enough people see what is wrong, and that it *is* possible to change things, the pressure for change will become irresistible.

> It is not the kings and generals that make history, but the masses of the people.
>
> Nelson Mandela

Godfrey Akorli, secretary of the Northern Poultry Farmers' Association. The IMF put pressure on the Ghanaian Government to reverse plans to impose a tariff on imported chicken.

Christian Aid/Penny Tweedie

chapter two

trade and development

why trade is not working for the poor

It is clear that trade is not working for poor people. Although the global economy as a whole has grown over the last 20 years, the economies of many poor countries have actually shrunk. While their share of world trade is tiny, trade for individual poor countries is actually a far more significant contributor to their national income than for most rich countries. Nearly a third of Africa's income[1] is accounted for by trade – a much higher proportion than for Europe or the USA. This means that the impact of international trade rules and policies tends to be far greater on poor countries than rich ones. For poor people living in these countries, smaller earnings from trade have meant less money to spend on food, clothing and school fees, and on investment to get them out of the cycle of poverty in which they are increasingly trapped.

Many of the poorest countries in the world are still living with the colonial legacy that has locked them into the production of one or two primary commodities – products such as coffee, copper, cocoa or timber, that are exported in their raw, unmanufactured state. Three-quarters of the least-developed countries are dependent on two or fewer commodity exports for over half their foreign exchange earnings. While earnings from some manufactured products, and services, have been rising continuously for many years, commodity prices are not only very erratic – rising or falling by more than 20 per cent in a year – but are also in long-term decline.

Unable to break into new markets and diversify their production, few of the world's poorest countries have been able to break out of this dependence.

Producers of these commodities in poor countries find it hard to move into producing other goods and cannot easily transfer into jobs in manufacturing or services. In too many cases other jobs are simply not available, or the social and personal costs of finding alternative employment are far too high. Most poor people lack the knowledge or resources to switch their production to other crops or to domestically produced, manufactured goods. In this situation, many poor producers facing declining prices and shrinking markets increase production as the only available way of maintaining their income. However, in a vicious cycle of poverty, this only floods the market even more and pushes prices lower.

Exporters from poor countries also find that they face increasing barriers when they process raw materials and try to export the resultant higher-value-added goods to industrialized countries' markets. This is partly because rich countries impose higher tariffs on more processed than unprocessed goods from developing countries, making them uncompetitive in rich countries. For example, European import tariffs on cocoa beans are 3 per cent, but can be as high as 27 per cent on processed chocolate. This is one of the major reasons why the four largest cocoa-producing countries (accounting for 90 per cent of the world market for cocoa) produce only 4 per cent of the world's chocolate. This is particularly important where, as in the case of chocolate, there is a widening gap between the prices paid for raw materials and the final consumer product. A box of chocolates costs 300 per cent more than it did 20 years ago, but the price of cocoa beans has actually fallen by 80 per cent over the same period.[2]

International trade rules are also preventing poor countries from providing sufficient support to producers to develop their processed-goods industries. For example, under the influence of conditions imposed by the World Bank, the Government of Mozambique was prevented from protecting its local cashew-processing industry between 1995 and 2000, forcing the country to remain dependent on exports of raw cashew.

All these problems affect people who are producing, directly or indirectly, for the international market. But trade is about imports as much as exports. The vast majority of people in the developing world produce for local markets, rather than for export. In many of the poorest countries, more than 70 per cent of the population rely on agriculture for a proportion of their income. Many of these people are subsistence farmers, producing primarily for their own consumption, with a small surplus to sell on the local market. This provides them with vital income for buying essentials that they cannot produce themselves, as well as paying for other important things such as education and medical treatment.

Over the past 20 years or so, international trade rules have had an increasing impact on such people. As poor countries have been required to open up their markets to international competition (as a condition for receiving loans from the IMF and World Bank – see below), small-scale farmers and producers in poor countries have faced growing competition from the highly mechanized, and often subsidized, farmers and industrialists in the developed world, and even from some larger developing countries. It is this growth in imports, rather than the lack of growth in exports, that is a key problem for many poor communities.

Many developing countries have seen their trade deficits grow because their export earnings have failed to keep pace with their import requirements. Recent research findings show that imports have grown up to four times faster than exports in some countries, after trade liberalization.[3]

The case of Fatima, the Senegalese onion farmer, has already been quoted in chapter one. Many other examples have been documented across the developing world. In Haiti, rice farmers were forced to leave their land in search of work when a sudden reduction in tariffs caused a flood of cheap, imported rice into local markets. In Ghana, tomato farmers in the poor Northern Region have lost their markets to imports of tomato paste from Europe. In Kenya, wheat farmers have seen prices tumble as a result of imported European wheat and, in Jamaica, dairy farmers are struggling to compete against imported milk powder.

Trade is vitally important to the development of countries and to the livelihoods of billions of the world's poorest people. At the moment, trade is failing many of the world's poorest countries. As a result of the long-term fall in commodity prices, the poorest countries that are dependent on such exports earn less each year for their labours. At the same time, many poor producers are being squeezed out of their local markets by cheaper and often subsidized rich country products. None of this is inevitable; ultimately it is a reflection of the fact that the current rules of trade are weighted against a great many poor people in too many poor countries.

what are the rules and who makes them?

Almost all international trade is subject to treaties and agreements between different countries. Historically, these agreements were predominantly bilateral (between two countries). These bilateral or regional trade agreements still exist today and can be very influential –

for example the North American Free Trade Agreement (NAFTA) between Canada, the USA and Mexico.

However, since the Second World War, a number of more far-reaching multilateral agreements have increasingly shaped the global trading environment and set the 'rules' that govern trade.

Since 1995, the World Trade Organization (WTO) has been the forum where most international trade rules are agreed. These rules are binding on all members (at least in theory – see below for further discussion) and its unique dispute settlement procedure can bring some of the world's most powerful countries and trading blocs to book. In this sense it plays a valuable role – and, as a defence against its many critics, it often points out that a system with no rules would be a free-for-all where poor countries would almost certainly be the major losers.

However, for the poorest countries in the world, the Washington-based International Monetary Fund (IMF) and World Bank probably have more influence than the WTO. Almost all the world's poorest countries rely on these institutions for financial assistance. By attaching conditions to this funding, the IMF and World Bank use their power to steer the countries' economic and trade policies.

These three organizations, and the rich country governments that wield influence through them, are responsible for setting what are often referred to as the 'rules' of international trade.

The thrust of the WTO agreements and the key conditions imposed by the IMF and World Bank push poor countries into adopting a set of economic policies known as 'liberalization'. This is the process of removing controls and restrictions on markets, including trade barriers, so as to create 'free markets', where goods and services can be freely traded within and across international borders. In practical terms this means that countries are required to reduce (and eventually eliminate) tariffs (taxes on imports and exports), quotas (limits on the quantities of a certain product that is imported or exported) and a range of subsidies provided to domestic producers.

The theory behind such policies is based on the belief that removing barriers and restrictions on markets will lead to an expansion in market activity, which, in turn, will enhance growth.

liberalization: blessing or curse?

After several decades when state intervention in the economy was the norm in both rich and poor countries, liberalization and free-market approaches became increasingly influential in the late 1970s and early 1980s. The rise of right-of-centre Governments in both the UK and the USA gave increasing influence to thinkers such as Milton Friedman, who had long been arguing that the state should withdraw from direct intervention in the economy and controls should be eased to let the private sector play a more prominent role.

It was argued that direct state intervention was inefficient because Governments lack crucial information and are prone to be either corrupt or influenced by narrow sectoral interests. In addition, civil servants lack the immediate incentives to make the right decisions that are faced by private-sector actors, whose jobs or investments are on the line. For all these reasons, and because of the poor performance of many developing countries after the impressive efforts of the 1960s, influential academics and a growing number of policy makers in donor countries, and in institutions such as the World Bank and IMF, argued that governments should seek to reduce their direct intervention in the economy and should focus on providing incentives for financial and economic markets to flourish.

In contrast to the inefficient state, it was argued that greater reliance on markets and market mechanisms would lead to a more efficient allocation of resources, leading to faster growth and poverty reduction.

The theory lying behind such beneficial outcomes is based on a number of crucial assumptions. These include 'perfect markets', which require that no single person or company can, by themselves, significantly influence prices or the average level of supply or demand, and 'perfect information', where everyone knows the available market price wherever they may want to buy or sell products.

> *However, these assumptions are far removed from the realities of our world and especially the realities of poor-country economies. In poor countries, many poor people cannot participate at all in some markets because they literally cannot get to the market in question or do not have the 'purchasing power' to buy what they need. Most fundamentally, an efficient distribution of resources does not necessarily mean a fair distribution.*

Under liberalization policies promoted by the WTO, IMF and World Bank, poor countries have reduced their import tariffs so that, in key sectors, they have more open economies than they have had in the past. However, liberalization policies implemented in developing countries have often not been matched and mirrored by such policies in industrialized countries. For example, the average tariff on imported agricultural products in developing countries is 20 per cent, while in developed countries it is 36 per cent.[4]

Researchers' attempts to provide a clear and unambiguous causal link between trade liberalization and higher growth, and higher growth to faster poverty reduction, have failed to show a clear relationship between the two. Prominent economists have described themselves as 'sceptical that there is a general, unambiguous relationship between trade openness and growth waiting to be discovered'.[5]

the WTO

The WTO is the newest of the institutions governing global trade. Established in 1995, it is 'directed to the substantial reduction of tariffs and other barriers to trade and to the elimination of discriminatory treatment in international trade relations'.[6]

The WTO is primarily a forum for trade negotiations between countries. Countries are free to join the WTO if they wish. With 146 member countries,[7] it is having an increasingly powerful impact on international trade. (A number of poor countries, such as Ethiopia and Tajikistan, have not joined.) The WTO monitors countries' implementation of agreements reached and is the forum where member countries can bring complaints against each other if those agreements are being violated. It can also authorize one country to impose sanctions on another, through the

Dispute Settlement Body. This enforcement mechanism makes it unique among international institutions, and is one reason why WTO agreements tend to override other international agreements.

Decision-making at the WTO is by consensus, with each member, in theory, having an equal say. However, in the past, powerful members such as the EU, the USA, Japan and Canada, have dominated negotiations, while poorer members have struggled to be heard. The result, with few exceptions, has been a set of rules and agreements biased in favour of the rich and powerful. Developing countries have had to fight hard to get any concessions to their particular needs. The UK negotiates at the WTO as part of the European Union.

Jamaica – undercut by cheap imports

For Jamaica the impact of us having signed on to the Uruguay Round agreement [that created the WTO] has been that we've lifted controls on beef, dairy, milk and so forth, and that has led to tremendous destruction of local dairy and local farmers who produce beef. Cheap meats that are very heavily subsidised from the US and Canada have come in and have decimated the local beef and dairy industry to the point where dairy farmers last year were actually having to throw away their excess milk. And these farmers are not subsidised; [they] are very small[-scale] farmers – men and women, heads of households – who are taking care of their families.

Mariama Williams, Caribbean Gender and Trade Network

a development round?

The WTO was set up following the final 'Uruguay Round' of negotiations of the General Agreement on Tariffs and Trade (GATT) in 1995. However, by the second ministerial meeting held in Seattle in 1999, tensions between members were already building. As protestors gathered on the streets outside, in the meeting a number of members (including key African countries) walked out, claiming that they were being excluded from important discussions and decisions.

In 2001, the WTO launched a new round of trade talks, dubbed the 'Development Round', at the fourth ministerial conference in Doha. The talks were meant to bring to the fore the needs and concerns of developing countries. In the event, procedural tricks, a lack of willingness to discuss key issues and the breakdown of trust between delegations led to frustrated progress.

Two years of missed deadlines and disagreement culminated at the ministerial conference held at Cancun in Mexico in September 2003. Once again, the conference was to break down without agreement. Developing countries were keen to see an agreement on agriculture but, instead, the EU and a few other countries insisted that a set of new issues should be added to the negotiating agenda. These issues – investment, competition, government procurement and trade facilitation – were ones that developing countries had repeatedly maintained should not be negotiated at the WTO as they were not central to the trade agenda.

Despite the failure to reach agreement at Cancun, the meeting may still prove to have been a turning point. The emergence of new alliances between developing countries, such as the 'G-20', may be a sign that the balance of power at the WTO is shifting. However, unless the EU and the USA agree to substantial reforms of their agricultural systems, and unless poor countries are guaranteed the right to intervene in trade where justified on development grounds, any resulting agreements will not have earned the right to be called a development round.

Despite persistent problems with the WTO process, a multilateral mechanism for discussing and agreeing international rules and agreements involving as many countries as possible is almost certainly the best way to structure trade rules in our increasingly global market. It may be that the only thing worse than a world with the WTO would be a world without a WTO but, of course, the rules have to be the right ones.

the World Bank and the IMF

Although they are not forums for negotiations, and in theory have little to do with the trading system, the IMF and the World Bank are probably the international institutions that have the greatest impact on the poorest countries' trade policies.

Much of the work of the IMF and almost all the work of the World Bank is focused on supporting the economies of the developing world. Yet both organizations are, in effect, run by the world's richest countries. Five countries (USA, UK, France, Germany and Japan) have more than 40 per cent of the votes and the 50 poorest countries have less than 3 per cent of the votes.

Both organizations have always laid down conditions for the loans they provide to poor countries. Among the prominent conditions set, especially since the early 1980s, were requirements that poor countries accelerate the process of liberalization of their economies. Many of these conditions were spelt out in World Bank structural adjustment programmes and IMF stabilization programmes. The aim was to open up economies, reduce intervention and regulation, and expose the economies of poor countries to the full force and influence of markets and market forces. The purpose of these programmes was to prepare the countries for higher growth and, ultimately, to a faster reduction in poverty levels.

Overall, however, the programmes failed to achieve their objectives in many countries, and especially in the poorest countries. Growth was lower than expected in most countries. Even where growth rates rose, faster poverty reduction often failed to materialize. In too many poor countries, unemployment levels continued to rise and incomes fell for many poor and vulnerable groups.

In a number of African countries, these policies led to a process of deindustrialization: factories closed, jobs were lost and what had been produced domestically was imported. Importantly, too, skilled artisans and engineers, on whom industrial development crucially depends, lost their jobs and many left their countries for work elsewhere. In Ghana, employment in manufacturing plunged from 78,700 in 1987 to 28,000 in 1993 after the local market was opened up to cheap consumer imports.[8]

These policies also affected trade and production of food and agricultural products. Tariff reductions led to a flood of imports. On the one hand, large numbers of farmers who had been selling products for both the domestic and export markets found themselves unable to compete with the imported goods and suffered significant income losses. Poorer farmers, who largely grew food crops for their own use but who were able to survive by selling seasonal crops, found that there was now no market, or severely reduced prices, for their products. Poor countries became more dependent for their food on imports, at a time when conflict, the effects of climate change on agricultural production, and poor and unreliable transport systems meant that countries should have been implementing policies to reduce, rather than increase, reliance on external suppliers to meet basic food requirements.

Countries were advised to produce more cash crops to earn foreign exchange to offset this problem but, in a number of instances, this only contributed to oversupply and a collapse in world prices for many products that are crucially important for poor countries, as occurred in the palm oil market.

What has been the effect of these policies on poverty? In the 1980s, only four developing countries saw reversals in terms of the Human Development Index (a summary measure based on living a long and healthy life, being educated and enjoying a sufficient standard of living). In the 1990s, that number had jumped to 21. Today, some 54 countries are poorer than they were in 1990: in 21 countries a larger proportion of people goes hungry; in 14, more children under the age of five are dying; and in 12, fewer children are enrolled in primary school.[9]

In 1999, the World Bank replaced its structural adjustment programmes with a new approach – poverty reduction strategies. On paper at least, these appeared to address a number of key concerns raised about the need for greater consultation and the need to focus on reducing poverty. However, in practice, serious problems have persisted. Development policies have tended not to be made for the country by the country, but instead seem to be strikingly similar to each other and to the views and approaches advocated by senior economists in these institutions. Involvement by the poor country concerned has often been reduced to minimal consultation with a lack of clarity about what impact these consultations might be expected to have.

Ghana: pressure to conform

The IMF are dictating to us instead of helping us to develop our national economy. The proposed tariff increase on imported chicken would have been just what we needed to help us develop and grow.

Godfrey Akorli, secretary of the Northern Poultry Farmers' Association

Since Ghana reduced its tariffs and opened its markets to more international trade, Ghanaian farmers have struggled to compete against cheap imports – many of them subsidized by either the US Government or the European Union.

In April 2003, the Ghanaian Government announced new measures to support their farmers by raising tariffs on imported chicken and rice. However, the tariff increases were never implemented as, within days of the announcement, opposition from the IMF had forced the government to drop its plans. It is easy to understand why the Ghanaian finance ministry was unwilling to reject the IMF's advice on the tariffs, as an earlier disagreement in 2002 had led to the IMF and World Bank labelling Ghana 'off track', and holding back money amounting to US$116 million.

What is important to note is that the IMF's action totally eclipsed Ghana's commitments under the WTO agreement on agricultural tariffs. Under this agreement, Ghana has the flexibility to raise its import tariffs to 99 per cent, but the IMF's action prevented Ghana from implementing an increase that would have resulted in a final tariff of less than 50 per cent.

Meanwhile, Ghanaian farmers struggle on, competing against cheap subsidized imports that threaten the very livelihoods they depend on.

negotiating with hands tied

IMF and World Bank trade policy conditionality applied on a country-by-country basis has another detrimental effect on poor countries: it undermines the little leverage poor countries have over other members of the WTO when they are negotiating new international rules and agreements. The pressures on individual countries to accelerate the opening up their domestic markets in the 1980s and 1990s effectively removed any bargaining chips that they might have used in trade-offs with other countries. Poor countries enter negotiations at the WTO having already implemented many of the liberalization reforms that the WTO is set up to negotiate.

regional and bilateral trade agreements

International trade negotiations are taking place alongside bilateral and regional trade negotiations and agreements. Bilateral and regional arrangements can mean very different things – from the level of integration practised in the EU, where there is free movement of goods and people, and even a common currency, to much weaker arrangements where countries come together periodically to discuss common issues.

There are advantages in countries, including poorer countries, coming together to form a single trading bloc. The larger market can encourage both domestic and international investment. If the economics are right, poor people can benefit from more trade between countries, as they have access to a wider range of goods at lower prices, and more opportunities to sell what they produce.

However, developing regional trading arrangements between groups of countries that are at different stages or levels of development can be problematic. This is because the larger and stronger members are able to exploit their strengths to attract the benefits to themselves, thereby obtaining greater gains. This can happen when groups of poorer countries develop regional arrangements, such as within the Southern Africa Customs Union, which is dominated by the South African economy. But it is particularly important when regional blocs encompass both rich and poorer countries. For instance, the North American Free Trade Agreement between Canada, the USA and Mexico may have brought more investment to Mexico's border towns, but at a very high cost. Mexico's poor farmers are now overwhelmed with cheap imports of maize, wheat and other products from the USA.

double standards and level playing fields

One of the greatest scandals of the current global trading system is that, while liberalization and market opening have been rigorously promoted and applied in poor countries, rich countries have written agreements in such a way that many of their own sectors continue to receive government support and protection.

The Common Agricultural Policy (CAP) subsidizes European farming to the tune of more than US$300 billion a year, either in the form of direct payments to farmers or subsidies to traders – to help them export excess production. The CAP additionally protects key sectors from international competition – many of which are of interest to developing country exporters. The fact that many of these measures benefit large agricultural businesses and big processing and trading companies disproportionately makes them even harder to justify. The USA, Japan and other developed countries also support their agricultural sectors in the same way.

These double standards increase inequalities between producers in rich and poor countries. Paying subsidies to producers and traders in rich countries makes it doubly difficult for poor producers to compete, even in their own markets.

The failure of rich countries to cut their subsidies and open their markets to the poorest countries is nothing short of a scandal. However, it would be wrong to conclude that, once rich countries have taken action in this area, the issue of trade justice will have been solved.

Although it is partly the trade policies of rich countries that have created the myriad of problems faced by producers in poor countries, the solutions do not lie only with rich countries. The WTO and supporters of rapid and far-reaching liberalization often advocate creating a 'level playing field' by cutting rich countries' subsidies and opening their markets to poor countries' exports. However, this will not enable poor countries to benefit from trade, as it does not deal with many of the fundamental problems facing poor countries, not least the relative power of rich-country traders to swamp poor-country traders and the need for poor countries to diversify their economies so that they can take advantage of the opportunities opened up by expanding world trade.

Even without subsidies, producers in rich countries will be in a much stronger position than most producers in developing, and especially the poorest, countries. Richer economies have had massive advantages in terms of technology, skilled labour, economies of scale, market intelligence and infrastructure.

In contrast, most poor countries lack the capacity to produce and supply the high-value products that consumers in rich countries demand. Achieving the necessary standards and breaking into these markets often requires the involvement of large international companies, many of whom are reluctant to share their technological and marketing expertise with others.

a level playing field?

International trade between my country and the West is like an antelope and a giraffe competing for food at the top of a tree. You can make the ground beneath their feet level, but the contest will still not be fair.

Dr Robert Abogye-Mensah, General Secretary of the Christian Council of Ghana

Many countries have no hope of competing in the globalised world – even assuming there is a level playing field – without help to get them to the point of self-sustaining development.

Joseph E Stiglitz, winner of the Nobel Prize for Economics 2001[10]

companies and their role

While trade rules are negotiated, agreed or imposed on countries, it is of course companies and individuals who actually do most of the trading. While companies have no formal role in making trade rules, it would be inaccurate to think of them as neutral bystanders. Liberalization policies have included measures aimed at removing many key restrictions that previously limited companies' scale and reach, enabling them to expand more rapidly into new markets around the world. In today's world, many companies are vast, multinational enterprises, with economic worth far greater than that of some countries.

Transnational companies play a powerful role in the global trading system. Their potential to benefit or to harm people in developing countries is enormous.

International business can provide investment, technology, jobs and market access to developing countries, enhancing incomes and helping economies diversify away from their dependence on primary commodity exports, for example cocoa or palm oil. However, size and influence should also be associated with transparency, accountability and responsibility, for these potential benefits are not guaranteed and the larger the company, the more able it is to manipulate its size and scale for its own internal interests and gains.

To address these concerns, large companies have advocated a growing role for self-regulation through what is termed Corporate Social Responsibility (CSR). The problem is that there is a gap, which appears to be growing, between the claims of companies that self-regulation is all that is needed and the reality on the ground. Around the world (and especially in poorer countries where company law is not as fully developed as in the industrialized countries, or compliance is lax) large companies are guilty of practices that violate human rights laws and conventions.[11]

Building on international human rights and environmental agreements, there is an urgent need for the international community to address moves toward internationally binding corporate regulation on CSR. This type of regulation could complement and work alongside voluntary initiatives. Where businesses are already operating at standards of best practice, these measures should surely be welcome.

corruption and trade

The opening up of markets, lowering tariffs and other key elements of the liberalization agenda have also been promoted on the assumption that they are an appropriate response to problems of corruption in developing countries. Corruption is undoubtedly a serious problem in many countries, both North and South, and very often it is the poorest people who pay the highest price for it. Clearly it needs to be addressed, and urgently.

However, the problems of corruption are complex and multi-faceted. The superficially attractive solution of 'leaving everything to the market' because this will eliminate the role of individuals, falls down in two major respects. Firstly, as already discussed, the functioning of markets in poor countries is far removed from the ideals of economic theory, and in reality can give individuals and companies enormous power. In this sense, it could be said that these markets are in some way 'corrupt'. Secondly, for corruption to be rooted out requires action on a range of fronts – within political, administrative and legal systems, across political processes and across countries. The most urgent need is to develop more rigorous and transparent systems of accountability of all key stakeholders – those within the private and public sectors and across civil society.

Liberalized economies continue to suffer from corruption in the way that more interventionist economies have in the past. In some cases, such as in the former Soviet Union, rapid liberalization can fuel corruption, presenting new opportunities for the corrupt and the criminal to exploit the system for their own ends.

how could poor countries gain more from trade?

The evidence over the last 20 years suggests that rapid and overarching liberalization policies have failed to generate the changes needed to achieve significant reductions in global poverty. If these policies have not been successful, the obvious question becomes 'what would work to enable poor countries to benefit more from trade, and to make trade a more effective driver for development and poverty reduction?'

Historical evidence suggests that trade liberalization has not, in the past, been associated with the same kind of success in terms of development and poverty reduction as has been the case in countries where governments have played some intervening role in the economy and been more flexible in their choice of trade policies. The experience of today's industrialized countries, and of some of the more successful developing countries, shows that a more 'managed' and interventionist trade policy has been key to growth and poverty reduction throughout both the nineteenth and the twentieth centuries. Careful government intervention in the economy and then the gradual opening up to world markets when economies were stronger and more able to compete has led to the development of stronger economies.

For example, the Model T Ford was developed in one of the most highly protected economies ever – the USA in the early twentieth century had an average import tariff rate of over 40 per cent for manufactured goods.

The success of the electronics industry in east Asia is another example. In South Korea, in the early 1960s and 1970s, small and emergent companies were provided with a range of incentives, including subsidies, and initially protected from competition with foreign firms. In return, they had to meet stringent requirements on export performance and were subject to domestic competition. In addition, the government invested heavily in developing a technology infrastructure, and in education and training, to create the conditions for high-technology export development to flourish.[12] This provided the groundwork for lowering tariffs at a later date, which led to higher growth in the domestic economy and the traded sectors. The key was ensuring that the incentives faced by both local and foreign companies encouraged innovation, export promotion and the development of new productive capacity and did not lead to stagnation and lower growth.

Mauritius provides an even more recent example of a successful economic development strategy. It shows that, even in recent times, governments that are able to be flexible in their choice of trade policies can break out of dependence on exports of a few primary commodities. By any standards, Mauritius has been successful in terms of both economic growth and poverty reduction. Growth per head averaged 4.2 per cent between 1975 and 1999, by which time per capita GDP was US$9,107. Productivity has also increased. Income inequality fell during this period, and life expectancy has increased by ten years.

These results were achieved through diversification away from almost total dependence on sugar exports to an economy based on services, manufacturing and agriculture. Diversification was not achieved through liberal economic policies. The IMF ranked Mauritius as one of the most protected economies in the world in the 1990s.[13] The key was targeted trade policy – giving incentives to exporters while protecting the labour force in the domestic sector from competition and providing a safety net for the population. While Mauritius benefited from preferential access to EU and US markets, unlike other countries with the same market access arrangements, it has employed the economic policy instruments to ensure that the country benefited over the long term.

However, this is not to say that protectionist and interventionist policies will always work. Such policies have also been associated with economies that have failed to diversify and grow, and with economies that have failed to lower the numbers of people living in poverty.

Latin America and African countries are usually cited as the clearest examples of inappropriate intervention. Though many of these countries sustained impressive growth rates and reductions in poverty for a number of years, especially in the 1960s, these were not sustained. A key problem in many cases seems to have been the lack of pressure put on those who gained from such protection. This meant that there was no incentive to use the advantages offered to develop new capacities. Benefits that were neither time-bound nor tied to performance requirements led to rent-seeking behaviour and expensive, poorly produced goods. In addition, the taxation of agriculture to fund industrial development limited agricultural growth and led to an increase in rural poverty in some cases.

trade justice economics: beyond liberalization vs protectionism

What all success stories in trade and development have in common is the ability of governments to manage trade in such a way that the incentives for business to create a profit and become more efficient steer them toward actions that promote development.

A closed system with no incentives has generally not worked to achieve economic growth and poverty reduction. However, it is equally true that open systems where restructuring is shaped more by external market forces have not had conspicuous success in fostering growth or poverty reduction.

What is needed is a system of trade rules that enables poor countries to prioritize the needs of poor people over any particular ideology. By its very nature, trade policy must be flexible – a 'one-size-fits-all' system can never work because of the sheer diversity of economic situations. But, by prioritizing the needs of people – both as economic and social beings – trade policies could begin to serve rather than to exploit or dominate. This new understanding might be termed 'trade justice economics', and would ensure that trade acts as a driver for development and for accelerating the push towards the end of mass global poverty.

making trade work for the poor

In the 1990s, Honduras, like many developing countries, implemented structural adjustment policies that resulted in the economy, by the IMF's definition, being one of the most open in the world. The changes had a devastating impact on some of the country's poorest people: production of rice in Honduras collapsed as farmers struggled to survive against cheap imports and falling prices. By the end of the decade, production levels were lower than 8,000 tonnes compared with a level of 50,000 tonnes reached in 1990. Both rice growers and the domestic processing industry were losing out, as most of the imported rice was ready milled.

Under pressure from local rice growers and the domestic processors, the government of Honduras decided it had to act. It has raised the tariff on processed rice and, in order to ensure that this benefits local farmers as well as processors, has drawn up an agreement whereby local processors are required to buy local rice first and then, if demand requires it, buy imported rice. While domestic rice is available the tariff on imported rice remains high. But, once local markets have been cleared, the rice millers can import unmilled rice at a very low 1 per cent tariff. This two-tiered tariff system appears to have succeeded on two fronts: local farmers have started to plant rice again, while rice consumers in Honduras have not faced significant price rises.

what can be done?

Trade offers the promise of a way out of persistent poverty for many developing countries and their people. But the benefits from trade are by no means automatic. Huge and glaring gaps remain between the potential and current realities.

The institutions that set the rules of trade and the rich countries that control them have promoted free-market policies and liberalization of poor countries' economies as the only way ahead. After more than 20 years of following such policies, the verdict is one of failure. Rich country interests continue to hold sway in agreeing international trade rules, which continue to bring greater benefits to rich rather than poor countries. We can and must do better for the world's poorest communities. For the Churches, this remains a matter not only of deep concern but also a question of justice.

Christian Aid believes that the UK Government can take significant steps towards trade justice for the world's poor:

- through the European Commission, support poor countries' proposals for more effective special and differential treatment in WTO rules and agreements – in particular this special treatment should aim to give poor countries the flexibility to support vulnerable producers and developing sectors as part of a nationally owned strategy for poverty reduction and development;

- support the reform of rich countries' agricultural subsidies to prevent the dumping of agricultural produce on poor countries' markets – an urgent priority should be the elimination of export subsidies;

- support the elimination of IMF and World Bank trade policy conditionality on the basis that these programmes limit the flexibility that poor countries have under current WTO rules and agreements and undermine their negotiating position in future trade rounds;

- ensure that any regional and bilateral trade agreements negotiated in the EU do not require poor countries to make liberalization commitments beyond what is required by WTO rules and agreements.

chapter three

trade justice:
a theological approach

starting from reality

Any theological understanding of trade justice has to start from the reality of trade and economics in the world today. That reality includes the fact that, while many people in the developed world are reaping the benefits of trade, millions in the developing world are losing out. This is not the outcome of misfortune or accident, but of a trading system, or 'trade rules', whose outcomes are deliberately skewed in favour of the already rich and powerful. This is contributing to global poverty, which has reached unprecedented levels, and a gap between the richest and poorest that continues to grow alarmingly.

This glaring injustice stands in stark contrast to the reality of God's nature, as revealed in Scripture and seen in Jesus Christ: a God who loves the world enough to become part of it and to enter into human life. The Christian vision is one of a world where all people are made in the image of God and are loved and valued in God's sight. Human life has been sanctified by Christ's incarnation. The world of trade and economics cannot be separated from the world of spirituality and faith.

Jesus' teaching is resonant with images from the economic life of his hearers: landless labourers search for work, merchants invest in land, farmers look forward to the harvest, shepherds search for their sheep, fishing communities worry about their catches. Jesus certainly saw no distinction between God's concern for people as spiritual and as economic beings.

However, in Christian tradition there has been a temptation to treat economics as somehow worldly and inferior to a concern for the life of the spirit. This idea sprang from platonic Greek philosophy and is entirely alien to the Jewish tradition of Jesus. Christians need to reaffirm that enforced poverty is contrary to the will of God and the Church is called to do all in its power to challenge it. As discussed further below, this response must

A Bolivian market seller. The Trade Justice Campaign reflects the Christian vision of a world where the needs of the poorest are met.

Christian Aid/S. Cytrynowicz

go beyond short-term and local responses to challenge the fundamental injustices of the structures that keep people in poverty. The Anglican Church worldwide has affirmed this 'transformation of unjust structures of society' as one of five 'marks of mission'.[1]

The urgent need to bring God's justice into the economic realm is a strong strand of biblical writing, particularly in the books of the law of the Old Testament. Clear within this teaching is the requirement that God's people must act in order to bring that justice about. This is most strongly seen in the 'jubilee' laws, which recognize that, unchecked by intervention, human greed will concentrate wealth in the hands of the few. So, every seventh and every fiftieth year are set apart as a time when the land is returned to its original owner, slaves are redeemed and debts are cancelled (Leviticus 25.8-55, Deuteronomy 15.1-2). Justice will not just come about on its own, or through the action of the 'invisible hand' of the free market, but time and again active application of the law is needed to enshrine the rights of the poor.

The 'poor' are often defined as widows, orphans and foreigners (outsiders to the community), three of the most marginalized groups in the society of the time. This preferential concern for the poor is an expression of the central core of God's new covenant, or relationship, with humanity. God identifies with the suffering of the people of Israel in slavery in Egypt and acts to liberate them. They must now reflect this relationship in their dealings with others.

For example, Exodus 22.21-27: 'You shall not wrong or oppress a resident alien, for you were aliens in the land of Egypt. You shall not abuse any widow or orphan … If you lend money to my people, to the poor among you … you shall not exact interest from them. If you take your neighbour's cloak in pawn, you shall restore it before the sun goes down …', and Deuteronomy 24.19-22: 'When you reap your harvest in your field and forget a sheaf in the field, you shall not go back to get it; it shall be left for the alien, the orphan and the widow … Remember that you were a slave in the land of Egypt; therefore I am commanding you to do this.'

Jesus called the poor 'blessed' (Luke 6.20), which has sometimes been used to justify doing nothing about poverty. But the experience of those working alongside poor communities affirms both that 'blessedness' through which poor people are able to be generous, resourceful and forgiving, and also the fact that living in poverty is debilitating and demanding. Enforced poverty diminishes and stunts people's God-given potential and can drive some to violence and despair.

The reality of the world today is that millions are forced to live in such poverty and, of even greater concern, this poverty, as outlined in the previous chapter, is being made worse for far too many by the global trading system as it currently stands.

It would be simplistic to state that poverty in the developing world is caused by wealth in the developed world. The interaction of global economic systems is far more complex than that. However, two things cannot be ignored: the reality of mass poverty in the developing world, and the fact that those who live in the wealthy world are benefiting from the same trading system that is harming their sisters and brothers in the global South.

For Christians in the rich world this could lead to different responses. We could become paralysed by guilt about a problem over which most of us would appear to have little direct control, and thus do nothing. This is often the path we take, either by choice or by apathy. We feel a vague concern, but become so overwhelmed by the scale of the problem that we actually fail to take any action at all.

A second response could be to realize and acknowledge that there are problems that need to be addressed, but to choose to assist merely by providing a little money to help those who remain poor by meeting their immediate needs. This kind of charitable response is a start and is clearly part of the gospel message to respond to those in need. But this type of response will do little to address the underlying problems and so will not provide the impetus for substantial change.

There is an alternative and third path: it starts by recognizing our own need for repentance. When we reflect that the world in which we live has been shaped by human hands, and that we have the power to change it, we can recognize God's call to participate in that change. When we acknowledge before God that our own greed and unwillingness to act are part of the problem, we can embark on the journey to begin to put right our failings. We do so in the knowledge of God's love and forgiveness, and God's desire that we should become the holy people we are called to be.

When we are able to repent of our own failings, then we can move forward, then we can respond to God's call to use the opportunities we have to pray and act for change. As Christians living in the UK, our relative wealth and power give us responsibilities that we need to take seriously.

St Luke's Gospel recounts an incident in the ministry of John the Baptist. When the crowds asked John what their response should be when they had been baptized, he said:

> 'Whoever has two coats must share with anyone who has none; and whoever has food must do likewise.' Even tax collectors came to be baptized, and they asked him, 'Teacher, what should we do?' He said to them, 'Collect no more than the amount prescribed for you.' Soldiers also asked him, 'And we, what should we do?' He said to them, 'Do not extort money from anyone by threats or false accusation, and be satisfied with your wages.'
>
> Luke 3.10-14

Each person is called to do what they can to make the world a more just place. Today, as citizens of one of the richest and still most powerful nations, Christians in the UK have a responsibility to use their influence on national leaders and to campaign for changes to the rules and institutions governing international trade.

> So that financial systems may no longer burden the poorest;
> so that nations may no longer grow rich at the expense of others;
> so that our trade may no longer trap people in poverty;
> God's kingdom come,
> God's will be done,
> on earth as it is in heaven. Amen.
>
> Peter Graystone (Christian Aid)

imagining a different world

From repentance, the assurance of God's forgiveness and the call to act for justice, Christians can begin to see how things could be different. In the tradition of the biblical prophets, the Church needs to be fearless in proclaiming that the world can be changed and in envisioning and building an alternative.

But what do the Bible and Christian tradition say about trade? If the current trading system is perpetuating and even causing poverty and inequality in the world today, can it be redeemed? Can trade be just and not exploitative?

There are many references to trade, in both the Old and the New Testaments. Often it is part of the backdrop or context to other teaching, rather than a commentary on trade in its own right.

However, an extended passage in Ezekiel and corresponding commentary in Isaiah (Ezekiel 28.1-19, Isaiah 23.1-17) describe the situation of the city of Tyre, one of the great trading cities of its time, around 600–500 BC. Tyre was positioned on a key trade route between the eastern Mediterranean and Asia and Africa. Ezekiel details the goods it traded: precious metals, slaves, bronze artefacts, horses, ivory, precious stones, fine linen, corn, honey, oil – and numerous other luxury goods (Ezekiel 27.12-24). They came from across the near east, north Africa and the Mediterranean. Ezekiel uses the appropriate metaphor of a richly built trading ship to describe how Tyre was shipwrecked at the height of its power and influence. He interprets this as judgement, not of trade per se, but of the pride of the King of Tyre, and of the oppressive and exploitative nature of Tyre's trade (Ezekiel 28.1-19).

The corresponding passage in Isaiah looks forward to a time when Tyre's trade will be just, and will serve the needs of people: 'Her merchandise and her wages will be dedicated to the Lord; her profits will not be stored or hoarded, but her merchandise will supply abundant food and fine clothing for those who live in the presence of the Lord' (Isaiah 23.18).

Among many early Christians, trade, like everything else, was seen in the context of an urgent expectation of Christ's return. At this time, Rome had taken over as the dominant trading power of the region, while individual converts – such as Lydia from Thyatira, 'a dealer in purple cloth' (Acts 16.14), and indeed Paul himself – presumably continued to practise their trade to support themselves and the Church. But concern for justice, in relation to poverty, continued: the letter of James echoes the prophets of the Old Testament in issuing warnings to rich oppressors, who exploit their workers (James 5.1-6).

In later Christian tradition, the ban on usury (interest charging) remained as an indication of the need for economic systems to avoid exploitation. After the Reformation, a far more positive theology of work and money-making emerged, often known as the 'Protestant work ethic'. However, it is worth noting that Calvin in particular opposed the abuses of excessive profits and proposed a series of measures to ensure that the poor were not exploited. While allowing usury, he included a rule that the poor should not pay interest and that excessive profit should be limited.[2]

Throughout its history the Church has had an uneasy relationship with trade and commerce. It has recognized its potential both for good, and for evil and exploitation. As the volume of international trade continues to increase exponentially, perhaps now is the time to consider this relationship again and to find a way of building a trading system that has justice and the needs of all people at its heart.

So is it possible to imagine a different world, where trade serves the needs of all people, and is prevented from being used as a tool for domination by a few? Perhaps one of the most important roles to be played by the Church is as a prophetic voice to remind the nation that the dominance of markets must be balanced by ensuring that they serve the needs of people.

The dominant neo-liberal ideology places great emphasis on free markets as the best way to determine economic efficiency. But, while Christians will want to recognize that market mechanisms do have a role to play, it is vital that their role is subordinate to the requirements of justice and equity for all God's people. The needs of the poor must come first – and the right to food, shelter, healthcare and education must be prioritized over adherence to a particular economic dogma.

This means that trade policy cannot be left entirely to the free market. We need to intervene to ensure that the weak as well as the strong benefit from trade. The neo-liberal economic model can no longer be seen as the only tool for trade policy. As outlined in the previous chapter, poor countries have been pushed into opening up to powerful market forces, through conditions imposed to gain vital IMF and World Bank grants and loans, as well as through WTO agreements. Concern for their impact on poverty has been at best secondary. This situation must be turned around – the needs of the poor must take priority because this is what justice demands.

building a eucharistic theology of trade justice

For millions of the world's poorest people, trade rules are increasingly determining whether they eat or go hungry. For a Church where the Eucharist is the central act of worship, how can a commitment to trade justice be understood in the light of this act?

The concept of the people of God gathering around the table to share bread and wine is central to the eucharistic service and, in that sharing, to participate in the life of Christ. We are the body of Christ, we receive his body, and we are sent out to be his body in the world.

Coming together in this way celebrates our oneness and rejects the individualism of much of our contemporary culture. At the offertory, our economic life is joined to our spiritual life in a central act of communion and community: the 'fruit of the soil and work of human hands' will become for us 'the body and blood of Jesus Christ'. We look forward to the kingdom where there will be enough to spare for all people and where 'all shall be included in the feast of life'.[3]

When Paul criticizes the Church at Corinth for abusing the Lord's Supper, it is because the Church has allowed divisions between rich and poor to be perpetuated in the Eucharist: 'For when the time comes to eat, each of you goes ahead with your own supper, and one goes hungry and another becomes drunk ... do you show contempt for the church of God and humiliate those who have nothing?' (1 Corinthians 11.21-22). This is the place where, above everywhere else, Christians are to be united.

This unity of rich and poor, oppressors and oppressed, gives Christians the confidence to campaign with, and on behalf of, each other. It overcomes divisions of geography, wealth or power that might otherwise separate and isolate different communities. Campaigning can become something that expresses the unity of the body of Christ.

Blessed are you, Lord God of all creation:
through your goodness we have this bread to set before you,
which earth has given and human hands have made.
It will become for us the bread of life.

Blessed are you, Lord God of all creation:
through your goodness we have this wine to set before you,
fruit of the vine and work of human hands.
It will become for us the cup of salvation.

Common Worship[4]

believing in the possibility of change

If as Christians we believe in the possibility of redemption and salvation, we must also believe that the world is not forever fixed in the way it does things. Real change is possible. As the Church, we must not only work for a world that better reflects God's justice, but must also believe that such a world can actually be built.

Although massive and rapid technological change now pervades people's lives, many either believe that actually 'nothing really changes' or are too bound up in the here and now to focus on what makes things so. Too many have become convinced that poverty is inevitable and that inequality is unchallengeable. This is tantamount to saying that God is powerless in our world. While, as Christians, we must be realistic about the fallen nature of human beings and the institutions we have created, we also know that 'for God all things are possible' (Matthew 19.26). History confirms that change is possible and does happen when people are prepared to act together to make it happen.

In the early years of the nineteenth century, committed Christians such as William Wilberforce and the 'Clapham sect' were pioneers in the struggle against slavery. In the face of considerable opposition, it took 18 years to win parliamentary support to abolish the slave trade and a further 26 years to end slavery in the British Empire.

The struggle against apartheid in South Africa seemed at times equally futile, yet leaders such as Archbishop Desmond Tutu refused to give up hope of their eventual success. 'Nothing,' he said, 'not even the most sophisticated weapon, not even the most brutally efficient policy, no, nothing will stop people once they are determined to achieve their freedom and their right to humanness.'

Campaigning for trade justice is a way of living a belief in the possibility of change. Christians can begin to put into action the prayer that God's kingdom will come and God's will be done on earth as in heaven.

> Hope unbelieved is always considered nonsense. But hope believed is history in the process of being changed.
> Jim Wallis[5]

Of course, campaigning is only one response to poverty. It is still important to respond to people's immediate needs, as the Church has been doing for many centuries. However, alongside a response of 'charity' must come a response of 'justice' that seeks to transform the underlying causes of people's poverty. It involves challenging the way the world is structured.

Together, campaigners work to bring about a transformation of the world. At the moment, the prevailing economic system idolizes acquisitiveness, power and valuing people for what they possess. This is in complete contrast to God's kingdom, where the last will be first and where people are valued for who they are, not what they have; where relationships of love, care, compassion and mutual interdependence are more important than profit and status.

Through campaigning, every person has a contribution to make and takes responsibility for bringing about that transformation. It is one way in which those who are often relatively powerless can reclaim their power and dignity under God. It is not the only way and it is not uniquely Christian. Christian campaigners will often find themselves working together with many who do not share their faith.

Non-violent, participatory campaigning, which empowers people in both rich and poor countries and believes in the possibility of change and transformation, offers a real chance to challenge the institutions and structures of power and wealth. For Christians, campaigners who speak out on behalf of the world's poorest people are acting as a sign of God's coming kingdom. Then all people, everywhere, will have a voice and will be heard; now, in a fallen world, Christian people need to speak out on behalf of each other.

As people whose life together is driven by prayer, Christian campaigners need to follow the advice often attributed to St Ignatius of Loyola: 'Pray as if everything depended on God; work as if everything depended on you.' Prayer that is passionate, real and demanding will align our will with God's will and bring together the urgent needs of the world with our willingness to be God's agents for change. It will lead us to live lives that are tireless in working for justice.

At the heart of the Lord's Prayer is the phrase 'Your kingdom come'. As this phrase is prayed each day the world over, Christians are called to live it out in many ways, of which campaigning is one. We live in an age where, possibly for the first time, we are able to envisage a world without poverty on the scale we see it today. By praying and campaigning together we have a real opportunity to bring about such a world.

> The Church of Jesus Christ is not called to be a bastion of caution and moderation. The Church should challenge, inspire and motivate people.
> The Kairos document, South Africa[6]

Trade justice campaigners meet with their MP outside the Houses of Parliament as part of the mass lobby for trade justice in June 2002.

Christian Aid/Elaine Duigenan

chapter four
the campaign: from fair trade to trade justice

introduction

How can the Church respond at all levels to the global situation of injustice in the way international trade is run? How can it respond to God's call to build a different world where the fulfilment of the rights of the poor and the promotion of human dignity are paramount?

The growing Trade Justice Campaign offers an opportunity to work with others within the Church, and with secular groups and those of other faiths, both nationally and internationally.

The campaign grew from small beginnings in 2000, as people looked around after the huge and significant Jubilee 2000 campaign for the cancellation of international debt. That campaign mobilized millions of people worldwide to call on governments and international institutions to cancel the backlog of unpayable debts owed by the world's poorest countries, as a celebration of the millennium. The Churches played a key role.

As the millennium year drew to a close, campaigners among a few UK development agencies began to ask the question, 'Where now?' How could the momentum of Jubilee 2000 be built upon in order to continue to tackle the blight of mass poverty in the world today?

The answer was clear – alongside debt, a fundamental, structural and economic cause of poverty in the world today is trade and the international rules that underpin it. In fact, trade is in many ways even more fundamental than debt – if it were not for the unjust patterns of trading that exist in the world today, the debt crisis would never have come about. And indeed, unless that injustice is tackled soon, many of the gains achieved by the Jubilee 2000 campaign will be lost through the perpetuation of current trade rules.

the fair-trade movement

Of course many people and groups, particularly within the Churches, are no strangers to the complex and unfair world of international trade. Since the 1970s, an increasingly influential 'alternative-trading' movement has been making steady progress. Traidcraft was set up in 1979 to offer poor communities in the developing world an alternative to reliance on aid, through participation in a positive trading relationship. Along with other similar organizations, it sought to model a different way of trading, in which both producer and consumer could benefit. It began by buying art and craft items from small producer groups and cooperatives in developing countries, and soon moved on to food products.

In the early 1990s the fair-trade movement faced a challenge: would it continue to concentrate on selling through catalogues, charity shops and at the backs of churches, or could it move into the mainstream and compete in the supermarkets, where so much of our food was sold? Taking its cue from the success of coffee certification schemes such as Max Havelaar in the Netherlands in 1994, Cafédirect coffee was launched. This was among the first of a range of products to carry the new Fairtrade Mark – awarded by the newly set up Fairtrade Foundation – guaranteeing that the product was produced and traded under certain criteria.

The Fairtrade Mark meant that consumers could be sure that the products they bought fulfilled minimum social and developmental standards. The fair-trade movement had learned lessons from the experience of 'eco-friendly' products in the 1980s, where there was no single accepted standard and, as a result, many products were marketed with 'green' claims that were not substantiated. Shoppers could trust the Fairtrade Mark.

In 1998 sales of Fairtrade Mark products in supermarkets and mainstream shops amounted to £16.7 million. By 2004, just six years later, they reached £100 million. Much of this success must be attributed to patient promotion and campaigning by caring individuals and groups – many of them in the Churches.

In March 2003, Chester became the first fair-trade diocese, pledging that at least 33 per cent of parishes would serve only fair-trade tea and coffee in their buildings. In fact 60 per cent agreed!

We hope that, in the years to come, this dramatic growth in sales of fairly traded products will continue, and these products become increasingly mainstreamed.

However, it is important to understand what buying fairly traded products does and does not achieve. Fair trade was developed as a practical response to the failings of the mainstream trading system. Specifically it was designed to help those disadvantaged producers who were marginalized from mainstream trade to be able to access international and local markets on fair terms. While fair trade is delivering significant benefits to poor producers, it is not the whole answer to systematic injustice in global trade.

The first simple reason is that not all products can carry the Fairtrade Mark. The Fairtrade Foundation and its international counterparts initially concentrated on certifying food products and are intending to move towards certifying manufactured goods, the first of which are fairly traded footballs.[1] In addition, members of the International Federation for Alternative Trade (IFAT), such as Traidcraft, sell products where a fair-trade label has not yet been developed.[2]

However, these goods form a small proportion of global trade. Fair trade assumes that the end consumer is in a position to make an ethical choice. This might not be the case with the vast majority of primary commodities, such as oil, iron ore and cement, which are traded around the world.

More significantly, at present, fair trade largely engages with problems faced by people in poor countries producing goods for sale in the rich world.[3] As outlined earlier in this report, the most serious impact of international trade can be on poor countries when they are forced into competing in their own local markets with well-resourced and often subsidized producers from the rich world. Fair trade cannot help a Haitian rice producer whose market has been undercut by sales of cheap rice produced in the USA.

The vast majority of the world's small-scale farmers produce not for the international market, but for their local market – and for the sake of the planet, this should surely continue to be the case. Where possible, trade should be local. Poor countries are faced with the problem that traders from rich countries are increasingly encroaching on those local or regional markets, with devastating consequences.

So, how should we see fair trade? First, it certainly helps those producers whose products are fairly traded. Communities across the developing world have been transformed by the additional security that selling through a fair-trade system brings. It offers financial security and guaranteed income, which can, and does, make a life-saving difference when commodity prices plummet. As the proportion of goods in the world market that are fairly traded increases, more and more communities will be able to benefit in this way. By strengthening them, fair trade gives them a stronger voice and opportunities for them to advocate for their needs with national and international policy makers.

Fair trade also has a vital symbolic value. By buying fair-trade products, consumers can show that they are prepared to put their money where their mouths are. It models a system that shows that trade can be a just exchange, where both trading partners can benefit. It is a powerful symbol of intent to build a trading system that puts the needs of the poor first. When, as a Church, we commit ourselves to fair trade, we show that we are prepared to put our belief in a more just world into action in a corporate way.

The fact that the UK public is prepared to spend £100 million a year on fairly traded products shows a widespread concern for economic justice, contributing significantly to a climate where these issues are taken seriously by policy makers. The fair-trade movement also draws on its practical trading experiences to enrich wider trade justice campaigns.

And finally, the fair-trade movement has played a vital role in raising awareness of the issue of international trade and, as members of the Trade Justice Movement, building the capacity of churches and others to be able to campaign on trade justice issues.

from fair trade to trade justice

Building on the twin foundations of the Jubilee 2000 campaign for debt cancellation and the fair-trade movement, the Trade Justice Campaign is calling for fundamental changes to the rules that govern international trade, so that they work in the interests of poor people. Without such radical change, trade will continue predominantly to serve the interests of the more affluent, and poor communities in poor countries will become increasingly economically marginalized.

notes

preface
1. World Bank, *World Development Report 2000.*

chapter one
1. *United Nations Development Programme Report*, 1999, pp. 36–38.
2. United Nations Conference on Trade and Development (UNCTAD), *Economic Development in Africa: trade performance and commodity dependence*, United Nations, 2004, p. 1.

chapter two
1. As measured by Gross Domestic Product (GDP).
2. Peter Robbins, *Stolen Fruit*, Zed Books, 2003.
3. A. Santos-Paulino and A. P. Thirlwall, *The Impact of Trade Liberalisation on Export Growth, Import Growth, the Balance of Trade and the Balance of Payments in Developing Countries*, University of Kent, 2002.
4. UNDP, *Making Global Trade Work for People*, 2003, p. 112.
5. Francisco Rodriguez and Dani Rodrik, *Trade Policy and Economic Growth*, Centre for Economic Policy Research, 1999.
6. The final act of the Uruguay Round, establishing the World Trade Organization.
7. As at 9 March 2004.
8. Sanjaya Lall, *Learning from the Asian Tigers: studies in technology and industrial policy*, Macmillan, 1997.
9. *UN Human Development Report*, 2003, p. 14.
10. *Financial Times*, 25 February 2004.
11. See *Behind the Mask: the real face of corporate social responsibility*, Christian Aid, 2004.
12. Lall, *Learning from the Asian Tigers*, 1997.
13. Arvind Subramanian and Roy Devesh, *Who can explain the Mauritian Miracle: Meade, Romer, Sachs or Rodrik?* IMF working paper, WP/01/116, 2001.

chapter three
1. '1. To proclaim the Good News of the Kingdom. 2. To teach, baptise and nurture new believers. 3. To respond to human need by loving service. 4. To seek to transform unjust structures of society. 5. To strive to safeguard the integrity of creation and sustain and renew the earth.' As developed by the Anglican Consultative Council, 1984–1990, and adopted by General Synod, 1999.
2. Christoph Stückelberger, *Global Trade Ethics*, WCC, 2002.
3. Christian Aid 50th birthday statement, 1995.
4. *Common Worship*, Church House Publishing, 2000, p. 291.
5. Jim Wallis, *The Soul of Politics: a practical and prophetic vision for social change*, The New Press and Orbis Books, 1994.
6. *Challenge to the Church: a theological comment on the political crisis in South Africa*, (the Kairos document), Braamfontein, Kairos Theologians, 1985.

chapter four

1. Currently the Fairtrade Mark covers twelve product categories (coffee, tea, rice, bananas, fresh fruit, juices, cocoa, sugar, honey, sports balls, wine, flowers).
2. Established in 1989, IFAT has over 200 members in 55 countries. Members are producer cooperatives and associations, export marketing companies, importers, retailers, national and regional fair-trade networks and financial institutions, dedicated to the fair-trade movement.
3. This is changing, however, as moves towards developing local fair-trade products in India, the Philippines and Kenya demonstrate that the model of trading fairly need not be confined to international trading relationships.
4. www.e-alliance.ch/pwa.jsp.
5. www.christianaid.org.uk/campaign.

how to communicate this report to your parish or synod

ten key points to make

- Poverty and inequality have reached unprecedented levels in the world. God's call for justice in the world requires the Church to respond.

- The way trade is managed is one of the fundamental contributors to this level of inequality. Current trade rules are weighted against the poor.

- Trade rules consist of deals negotiated at the World Trade Organization (WTO); conditions and policy advice set by the International Monetary Fund (IMF) and World Bank; and trade agreements made between groups of countries: all these are strongly influenced by rich countries.

- The rules demand that poor countries open their markets and reduce the amount of help they give to their own producers and industries – this process is called liberalization. It throws poor communities into competition with the rich and powerful.

- Evidence suggests that such liberalization is not always the best way to reduce poverty. Neither is blanket protectionism. What is needed is a new economic system of trade justice that ensures that trade rules should prioritize the needs of poor people.

- The Bible criticizes trade where it exploits the poor, and teaches that intervention is often needed to bring about justice.

- Christian faith teaches that transformation is possible and that Christians all have a role to play in bringing about change. This process has to start with repentance.

- One response to the current situation is to buy Fairtrade Mark products. This benefits the producers and models an alternative way of trading.

- As well as buying fair products, it is vital to campaign to change trade rules. This is the only way in which more fundamental and far-reaching change will come about.

- 2005 has the potential to be a significant year – when campaigners will have the opportunity to make their case to the UK Government, and to join together in a Week of Action from 10 to 16 April 2005.

suggestions for action

- Parishes can encourage their congregations to pray and campaign for trade justice. Campaign resources are available from member organizations of the Trade Justice Movement (see list below). Activities might include sending campaign postcards, taking part in joint actions (e.g. *Sponsored by Letters*, Vote for trade justice) and by attending campaign events.

- The Week of Action for trade justice, 10–16 April 2005, will provide an opportunity for activities in support of the campaign, locally and internationally, in advance of the UK presidency of the G8 and the EU.

- Wearing a trade-justice badge raises awareness of the campaign. Badges cost £2 (plus p&p) and may be ordered by telephoning 01252 669628.

- Parishes and dioceses can continue to support the buying of Fairtrade Mark products, as a sign of their visible commitment to a more just and equitable trading system. Dioceses can use the process of becoming a 'fair-trade diocese' to involve the church membership at all levels, to educate and campaign for trade justice.

- PCCs, deanery and diocesan synods can debate the campaign and pass a resolution in support.

- The Church could play a key role in building international support for the campaign within the Anglican Communion, and through contacts mediated by mission agencies, development agencies and diocesan links.

resources and further reading

useful free resources from Christian Aid

Order these free items from Christian Aid by telephoning 08700 787 788 and quoting the relevant code.

Action Request (ask for the latest issue) – keep up to date with the campaign and take easy but effective actions five times a year.

Writing the wrongs: write letters for trade justice (F697) – who to write to and what to say.

Play Unfair! How to hold an unfair games (F759) – a fun way to publicize the Trade Justice Campaign and keep the issue on the Government's agenda.

Sponsored by Letters action pack (F822) – everything you need to encourage your church or local group to get involved in effective action to support the Trade Justice Campaign.

How to pass a trade justice resolution (F672) – sample wordings and tips for action.

Lifting the burden, weighting the rules: faith foundations for the Trade Justice Campaign (F791) – theological background to the campaign.

Trade Justice: what's it to you? (F911) – free ten-minute video that introduces the campaign and explains how to get involved, featuring Kwame Kwei-Armah, from BBC TV's *Casualty*.

useful contacts
for further information

CAFOD
2 Romero Close, London, SW9 9TY
www.cafod.org.uk

Christian Aid
PO Box 100, London, SE1 7RT
Visit www.christianaid.org.uk or telephone 020 7523 2225 for further information, to ask to receive campaign mailings or for details of your local Christian Aid office.

Tearfund
100 Church Road, Teddington, Middlesex, TW11 8QE
www.tearfund.org

The Fairtrade Foundation
Suite 204, 16 Baldwin's Gardens, London EC1N 7RJ
www.fairtrade.org.uk

Traidcraft
Kingsway, Gateshead, Tyne and Wear, NE11 0NE
www.traidcraft.co.uk
All the above organizations are members of the Trade Justice Movement. For a full list of members see www.tjm.org.uk/members.shtml.

suggested further reading

Chang, Ha-Joon, *Kicking Away the Ladder: development strategy in historical perspective*, Anthem Press, 2002.
Curtis, Mark, *Trade for Life*, Christian Aid, 2001.
Madeley, John, *Hungry for Trade: how the poor pay for free trade*, Zed Books, 2000.
Reed, Charles (ed.), *Development Matters: Christian perspectives on globalization*, Church House Publishing, 2001.
Stiglitz, Joseph, *Globalization and Its Discontents*, Penguin, 2003.
Stückelberger, Christoph, *Global Trade Ethics: an illustrated overview*, WCC Publications, 2002.
UNDP, *Making Global Trade Work for People*, Earthscan, 2003.